SEASONS

Summer

by Ann Herriges

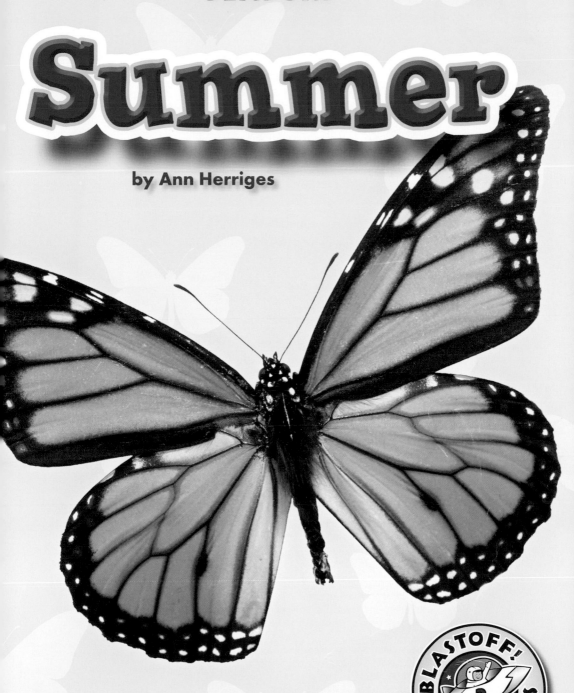

BELLWETHER MEDIA • MINNEAPOLIS, MN

Note to Librarians, Teachers, and Parents:

Blastoff! Readers are carefully developed by literacy experts and combine standards-based content with developmentally appropriate text.

Level 1 provides the most support through repetition of high-frequency words, light text, predictable sentence patterns, and strong visual support.

Level 2 offers early readers a bit more challenge through varied simple sentences, increased text load, and less repetition of high-frequency words.

Level 3 advances early-fluent readers toward fluency through increased text and concept load, less reliance on visuals, longer sentences, and more literary language.

Whichever book is right for your reader, Blastoff! Readers are the perfect books to build confidence and encourage a love of reading that will last a lifetime!

This edition first published in 2007 by Bellwether Media.

No part of this publication may be reproduced in whole or in part without written permission of the publisher. For information regarding permission, write to Bellwether Media Inc., Attention: Permissions Department, Post Office Box 1C, Minnetonka, MN 55345-9998.

Library of Congress Cataloging-in-Publication Data
Herriges, Ann.
  Summer / by Ann Herriges.
    p. cm. — (Seasons) (Blastoff! readers)
Summary: "Simple text and supportive images introduce beginning readers to the characteristics of the season of summer. Intended for students in kindergarten through third grade."
  Includes bibliographical references and index.
  ISBN-10: 1-60014-032-7 (hardcover : alk. paper)
  ISBN-13: 978-1-60014-032-7 (hardcover : alk. paper)
  1. Summer—Juvenile literature. I. Title. II. Series.

QB637.6.H47 2007
508.2—dc22   2006000613

Text copyright © 2007 by Bellwether Media.
Printed in the United States of America.

Table of Contents

Summer is here! Summer is the **season** that comes after spring.

Days are long in summer. The sun rises early in the morning and sets late at night.

The sun climbs high in the sky. The **sunshine** is strong.

Summer weather is warm.
Sometimes the air feels
heavy and wet.

A **heat wave** can bring many
days of hot and sticky weather.

Then storms rumble in. **Thunder** booms! **Lightning** flashes! Rain falls from the clouds.

The sunshine and rain make plants grow. Grass is thick and green.

Trees are full of leaves.
Gardens burst with vegetables.

Farmers mow tall grass to make **hay**. Crops grow tall in the fields.

Flowers are in **bloom**.

Animals are busy in summer.
Bees and butterflies drink
nectar from flowers.

Spiders spin **webs**. Caterpillars chomp on leaves.

Baby birds learn to fly.
Ducklings start to swim.

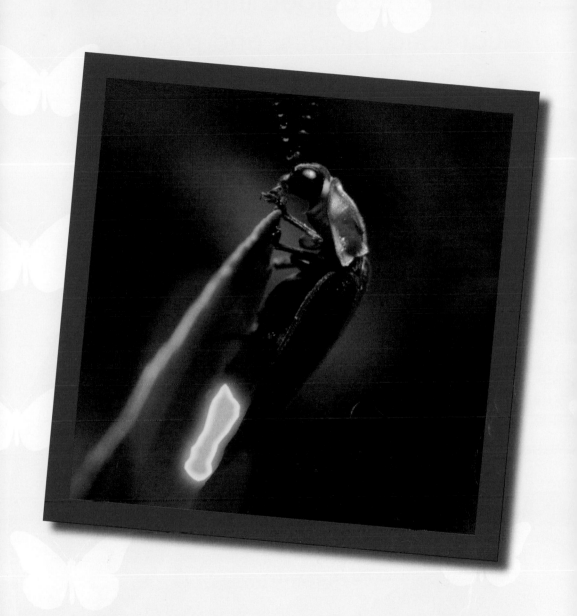

Bats swoop in the sky at night.
Fireflies glow in the dark.

Summer is a good time for camping, picnics, and parades.

You can cool off in the **shade** or in the water.

You can lie in the soft grass and watch the clouds float by.

Finally the air grows cooler. The sun sets earlier. Soon summer will be gone and it will be fall.

Glossary

bloom—when a flower grows and opens

hay—grass that is dried and fed to horses and other farm animals

heat wave—very hot weather that lasts for several days in a row

lightning—electricity in the sky that makes a flash of light, usually during a thunderstorm

nectar—a sweet liquid in flowers that some insects drink; bees collect nectar and make it into honey.

season—one of the four parts of the year; the seasons are spring, summer, fall, and winter.

shade—an area that is sheltered from the light; it is shady under trees and umbrellas.

sunshine—rays of light from the sun

thunder—the loud sound that comes after a flash of lightning; the lightning heats the air until it explodes as thunder.

web—a net of sticky threads that a spider makes to catch insects for food

To Learn More

AT THE LIBRARY
Kelley, Marty. *Summer Stinks*. Madison, Wisc.: Zino Press Children's Books, 2001.

Payne, Nina. *Summertime Waltz*. New York: Farrar, Strauss, and Giroux, 2005.

Plourde, Lynn. *Summer's Vacation*. New York: Simon & Schuster, 2003.

Rockwell, Anne. *Four Seasons Make a Year*. New York: Walker, 2004.

ON THE WEB
Learning more about the seasons is as easy as 1, 2, 3.

1. Go to www.factsurfer.com

2. Enter "seasons" into search box.

3. Click the "Surf" button and you will see a list of related web sites.

With factsurfer.com, finding more information is just a click away.

Index